ZOMBIE-GUT CHILI

and Other HORRIFYING DINNERS

Ali Vega

Lerner Publications ◆ Minneapolis

Lerner Publications Company
A division of Lerner Publishing Group, Inc.
241 First Avenue North
Minneapolis, MN 55401 USA

For reading levels and more information, look up this title at www.lernerbooks.com.

Main body text set in Tw Cen MT Std.
Typeface provided by Monotype.

Library of Congress Cataloging-in-Publication Data

Names: Vega, Ali, author.
Title: Zombie gut chili and other horrifying dinners / by Ali Vega.
Description: Minneapolis : Lerner Publications, [2016] | Series: Little kitchen of horrors | Audience: Ages 7-11. | Audience: Grades 4 to 6. | Includes bibliographical references and index.
Identifiers: LCCN 2016018648 (print) | LCCN 2016020247 (ebook) | ISBN 9781512425734 (lb : alk. paper) | ISBN 9781512428094 (eb pdf)
Subjects: LCSH: Dinners and dining--Juvenile literature. | Cooking--Juvenile literature. | LCGFT: Cookbooks.
Classification: LCC TX737 .V44 2016 (print) | LCC TX737 (ebook) | DDC 641.5/4--dc23

LC record available at https://lccn.loc.gov/2016018648

Manufactured in the United States of America
1-41341-23285-8/23/2016

Photo Acknowledgments
The images in this book are used with the permission of: © Yuri_Arcurs/iStockphoto, p. 4; © Mighty Media, Inc., pp. 5 (top left), 5 (top right), 5 (bottom), 9 (left), 9 (right), 10, 11 (top), 11 (middle), 11 (bottom), 12, 13 (top), 13 (middle), 13 (bottom), 14, 15 (top), 15 (middle), 15 (bottom), 16, 17 (top), 17 (middle), 17 (bottom), 18, 19 (top), 19 (middle), 19 (bottom), 20, 21 (top), 21 (middle), 21 (bottom), 22, 23 (top), 23 (middle), 23 (bottom), 24, 25 (top), 25 (middle), 25 (bottom), 27 (top), 27 (middle), 27 (bottom), 28, 29 (top), 29 (middle), 29 (bottom); © Elena Elisseeva/Shutterstock Images, p. 6; © Ronnachai Palas/Shutterstock Images, p. 7; © Monkey Business Images/ Shutterstock Images, p. 8; © Fertnig/iStockphoto, p. 30.

Front Cover: © Mighty Media, Inc.

CONTENTS

Introduction

DREADFUL DINNERS

What is your favorite dinner? Perhaps stuffed peppers are your pick. Or maybe it's gooey macaroni and cheese. But what if those peppers oozed puke all over your plate? Would you eat mac and cheese if it had flakes of crusty monster skin mixed in? The answer is yes, if your dish was as tasty as it was terrifying!

Many people delight in being frightened by food. Revolting recipes are tons of fun to make, serve, and eat. From meat loaf with onion fingernails to dumplings that look like dissected brains, getting grossed out by food is just plain fun. So put on your apron, and prepare to horrify hungry friends and family members with disgusting and delicious dinners!

Before You
GeT STaRTeD

Cook Safely! Creating disgusting dinners means using many different kitchen tools and appliances. These items can be very hot or sharp. Make sure to get an adult's help whenever making a recipe that requires use of an oven, stove, or knife.

Be a Smart Chef! Cooking gross dinners can be messy. Ask an adult for permission before starting a new cooking project. Then make sure you have a clean workspace. Wash your hands often while cooking. If you have long hair, be sure to tie it back. Make sure your guests don't have any food allergies before cooking. Adjust the recipes if you need to. Make sure your gag-worthy dinners are safe to eat!

Tools You'll Need

Cooking can involve special tools and appliances. You will need the following items for these disgusting recipes:

- freezer
- oven
- refrigerator
- slow cooker or crockpot
- stove or hot plate

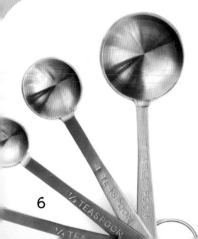

METRIC CONVERSION CHART

Use this handy chart to convert recipes to the metric system. If you can't find the conversion you need, ask an adult to help you find an online calculator!

STANDARD	METRIC
¼ teaspoon	1.2 milliliters
½ teaspoon	2.5 ml
¾ teaspoon	3.7 ml
1 teaspoon	5 ml
2 teaspoons	10 ml
1 tablespoon	15 ml
¼ cup	59 ml
⅓ cup	79 ml
½ cup	118 ml
⅔ cup	158 ml
¾ cup	177 ml
1 cup	237 ml

150 degrees Fahrenheit	66 degrees Celsius
300°F	149°C
350°F	177°C
400°F	204°C

1 ounce	28 grams
1 fluid ounce	30 milliliters
1 inch	2.5 centimeters
1 pound	0.5 kilograms

DISGUSTIFYING YOUR DINNERS

Nasty Names

A good gross-out name can change an everyday **edible** into something nasty. Once a dish is given a gross name, your diners will have a hard time picturing it as anything else! Onions become fingernails, and ketchup turns into blood. Cooked rice really looks like maggots. And spaghetti noodles are greasy strands of hair!

As you cook, examine your ingredients. Do any inspire you to call them by nauseating names? You could make a fun label to display with your food. And make sure to announce the terrible title of each dinner dish you serve. Your guests' looks of horror are half the fun!

Sickening Setups

A supergross name is the key to a truly disgusting dinner. But the way you present your horrifying dishes is also important. Use fun props to make your meals seem extra revolting. It might be funny to have a saw on the table when you serve your monster-hand meat loaf. A clean pair of nail clippers might be a nice touch too. Fake bugs and bandages will make your dinners extra horrifying. Whatever props you use in your presentation, make sure they are **sanitized**. Keep things delicious, safe, and fun.

ZOMBIE-GUT CHILI

Oozing zombie entrails and blood clots are what's for dinner!

Ingredients

1 14-ounce package bratwurst
2 15-ounce cans great northern beans, drained
2 15-ounce cans chicken broth
2 cans whole peeled tomatoes, including the juice
2 cloves **minced** garlic
1 teaspoon oregano
1 teaspoon cumin
1 teaspoon chili powder
1 4-ounce can green chilies
½ teaspoon salt
1 teaspoon pepper
sour cream
food coloring in several colors

Tools

• measuring spoons
• slow cooker or crockpot
• mixing spoons
• knife
• cutting board
• small bowls
• serving bowls

Serves: 6
Preparation Time: 3½–8½ hours (30 minutes active)

1. Put all the ingredients except the sour cream and food coloring in the slow cooker.

2. Turn the slow cooker to the low setting, and cook for 7 to 8 hours. Or cook on high for 3 to 4 hours.

1

3. Stir everything together with a big spoon.

4. Carefully remove the bratwurst, and chop it into sections. Then put it back in the slow cooker for 15 more minutes.

4

5. Put several spoonfuls of sour cream in each small bowl. Add several drops of food coloring to each bowl and stir in. For an extra-gross look, combine two colors, but don't mix completely. This create swirls.

6. Scoop the chili into serving bowls. **Garnish** with the sour cream, and enjoy some zombie-gut ooze.

5

TIP

If you don't have a slow cooker, you can make this chili using a large stockpot on the stove. Bring all ingredients to a boil, and simmer for 1 hour.

SLIMY WITCHES' HAIR SPAGHETTI

Twirl this greasy tangle of witches' hair and tomato scabs on your fork!

Ingredients

1 pound angel-hair pasta
½ cup plus 1 tablespoon olive oil
4 cloves minced garlic
1 teaspoon Italian seasoning blend
1 tablespoon dried basil
1 14½-ounce can diced tomatoes
¼ teaspoon salt
¼ teaspoon pepper
4 tablespoons grated Parmesan cheese

Tools

- large stockpot
- colander
- measuring spoons
- small glass
- large bowl
- food coloring in several colors
- mixing spoons
- serving plates

Serves: 4
Preparation Time: 1 hour

1. Fill the stockpot three-quarters full with water. With an adult's help, bring the water to a boil over medium-high heat. Add the pasta, and cook according to the package directions.

2. When the pasta is done, put 3 tablespoons of pasta water in a small glass. You will use this water later! With an adult's help, drain the pasta using a colander.

3

3. Fill a large bowl halfway with water. Add several drops of each color of food coloring to dye the water black. Then soak the pasta in the water for 15 to 20 minutes. Drain the pasta one more time, and mix with ½ cup olive oil.

4. In the clean stockpot, heat the remaining oil over medium heat. Add the garlic, and cook about 1 minute.

5. Add the Italian seasoning, basil, and tomatoes to the oil and garlic mix. Then add the salt and pepper, and cook for 5 minutes.

5

6. Add the pasta and pasta water to the pot. Then stir together for 1 minute until heated through. Swirl pasta on each plate, and garnish each serving with 1 tablespoon Parmesan cheese. Now serve up your slimy hair!

6

PUKING PEPPERS

Bake pepper people who puke up a gross-looking mix of cheesy ground beef!

Ingredients

1 pound ground beef
1 14½-ounce can diced tomatoes
½ 14½-ounce can corn
½ 14½-ounce can pinto beans
½ teaspoon salt
¼ teaspoon pepper
1 teaspoon chili powder
½ teaspoon onion powder
½ teaspoon garlic powder
3–4 bell peppers
¾ cup shredded cheese

Tools

- frying pan
- mixing spoons
- measuring spoons
- knife
- cutting board
- baking pan
- oven mitts
- serving plates

Serves: 4
Preparation Time: 45 minutes

1. **Preheat** the oven to 350°F. Brown the ground beef in the pan, stirring constantly. Add the tomatoes, corn, beans, salt, pepper, chili powder, onion powder, and garlic powder. Mix well, and remove the pan from heat.

1

2. Have an adult help you cut off each pepper's top. Set the tops aside. Then scoop out each pepper's innards and discard. Make two small slits in each pepper for eyes. Then cut one longer slit for a mouth.

3. Stand each pepper upright on the baking pan. Spoon the ground beef mixture into each one. Sprinkle cheese on top, and then replace the peppers' tops.

2

4. Bake the peppers for 15 to 20 minutes. Remove from oven, and plate each pepper.

5. Have an adult help you cut each eye slit to make it wider. Then cut each mouth slit from the corners all the way down to the plate. Pull the mouths open, and watch the "puke" ooze out. Your sickly peppers are ready to serve!

3

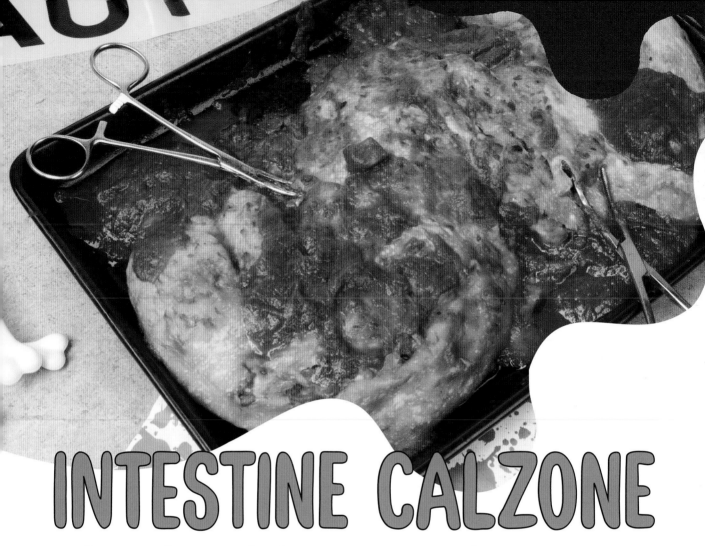

INTESTINE CALZONE

Cook up a slimy coil of oozing intestines!

Ingredients

1 13.8-ounce package ready-made pizza
    dough
¾ cup shredded Monterey Jack cheese
½ onion
1 8-ounce can black olives
1 24-ounce jar pizza or pasta sauce

Tools

- rolling pin
- baking sheet
- measuring cups
- knife
- cutting board
- spoon
- oven mitts

Serves: 4
Preparation Time: 45 minutes

1. Preheat the oven to the recommended temperature on the pizza dough package.

2. Roll out the dough into a large rectangle on a baking sheet.

3

3. Sprinkle the cheese over the dough.
Chop the onion and olives, and sprinkle on top of the cheese. Then add about half of the sauce, and set the rest aside.

4. Carefully roll the dough into a log with the toppings inside. Pinch the log's ends together.

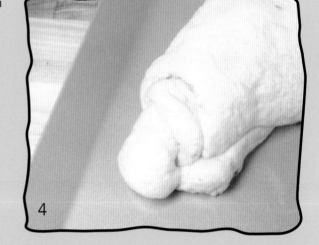

4

5. Place the log on the baking sheet. Arrange the log so it makes a zigzag shape. It should look like an intestine! Bake the pizza dough according to the package directions.

6. Remove from the oven, and add the remaining tomato sauce along the calzone's edges. It should look like gooey, oozing blood! Yum!

5

TIP

Add bits of Italian sausage or bacon to the filling for a fleshier flavor!

MONSTER-SKIN MAC AND CHEESE

An ooey, gooey pasta packed full of peeling, oozing monster skin. Watch out for warts!

Ingredients

½ cup (1 stick) butter

⅔ cup flour

2 cups whole milk

¼ teaspoon salt

½ teaspoon pepper

3 cups shredded cheddar cheese

1 cup shredded Parmesan cheese, plus a little extra for garnish

1 pound elbow pasta

8 ounces cubed smoked ham

cooking spray

4 slices cooked and chopped bacon

capers or green peas

Tools

• measuring cups

• large saucepan

• mixing spoons

• measuring spoons

• **whisk**

• large stockpot

• colander

• large baking dish

• oven mitts

Serves: 4
Preparation Time: 45 minutes

1. Preheat the oven to 350°F. Melt the butter in the bottom of a large saucepan over medium heat. Add the flour, and stir for 3 minutes over low heat.

2. Turn the heat up to medium, and add the milk. Cook until thickened, about 5 to 8 minutes. Add the salt and pepper.

3. Turn off the heat, and whisk in the cheddar cheese. Then add 1 cup of Parmesan cheese. This makes a sauce.

4. Cook the pasta in a stockpot according to the package directions. With an adult's help, drain the pasta using a colander. Then combine the pasta, cheese sauce, and ham in the stockpot, and mix together.

5. Coat the baking dish with cooking spray, and pour in the pasta mixture.

6. Sprinkle the pasta with bacon and extra Parmesan cheese. Bake for 25 to 30 minutes. When your monstrous mac and cheese is done, add caper or green pea warts for some ferocious flair!

TIP

Add Weenie Witch Fingers from page 16 of *Witches' Brew and Other Horrifying Party Foods* for an extra gross garnish.

MAGGOT BURGERS

Make burgers swarming with squirming maggots.
Eat up before they hatch!

Ingredients

1 cup uncooked rice
1 pound ground turkey or beef

Burger Seasoning
¼ teaspoon salt
1½ teaspoons paprika
1½ teaspoons garlic powder
¼ teaspoon cumin
1 teaspoon ground black pepper
¾ teaspoon dried basil
¾ teaspoon dried parsley
¼ teaspoon chili powder
½ teaspoon onion powder
4 slices white cheddar cheese

4 hamburger buns
ketchup for serving

Tools

• medium saucepan
• measuring cups
• baking dish
• measuring spoons
• mixing bowls
• mixing spoon
• broiling pan
• oven mitts
• spatula
• fork

Serves: 4
Preparation Time: 30 minutes

1. Cook the rice in the saucepan according to the package instructions. Put ½ cup of cooked rice into a small bowl. Put the rest of the rice into a baking dish. Then preheat the oven to the **broil** setting for 5 to 10 minutes.

2

2. Mix together the burger seasoning ingredients in a small bowl. Then mix the ground meat with the seasoning, and form four patties using clean hands.

3. Roll each patty through the rice in the baking dish. The rice should stick to the patty in some places but not everywhere.

3

4. Gently place the patties in the broiling pan, and place it in the oven. Cook for 6 to 7 minutes.

5. Remove the pan from the oven. Then flip the patties, and broil another 1 to 2 minutes.

6. Place a slice of cheese on each bun bottom, then add the patties. Pierce the patties with a fork to let some juices ooze out. Then add a little more rice from the bowl you set aside in step 1. Add the bun tops, and serve the burgers with ketchup. Can you see your maggots wiggling?

6

BACON-WRAPPED WORM

Cut into this massive meat worm before it takes a bite out of you!

Ingredients

1 1-pound pork tenderloin
8–10 bacon slices
1 apple
2 pearl onions, peeled
pimientos
greens or tomato sauce for serving

Serves: 4
Preparation Time: 4–5 hours
(30 minutes active)

Tools

- cutting board
- plastic wrap
- baking dish
- oven mitts
- tongs
- meat thermometer
- knife
- toothpicks

1. Lay the pork tenderloin on a piece of plastic wrap. Cover the pork with strips of bacon. The strips should overlap one another, so they completely cover the tenderloin. This is your worm's body.

2. Wrap the pork and bacon in plastic wrap. Place in the freezer for 3 hours. (Bacon cooks faster than tenderloin. Freezing first evens out the cooking time.)

3. Remove the pork from the freezer, take off the plastic wrap, and place in a baking dish. Preheat the oven as needed, then bake your worm according to the instructions on the tenderloin package.

4. Use tongs to flip the worm over. Then bake for 10 more minutes, and check for doneness.

5. Remove the pork from the oven, and allow to cool. Then, with an adult's help, cut out the worm's mouth. Add an apple slice for a spooky smile. Use toothpicks to attach onion eyes with pimiento pupils.

6. Serve the worm on a bed of greens or in a puddle of tomato sauce. Disgusting!

1

2

TIP

5

Use a meat thermometer to check if your pork is done. Pork is cooked when it is between 145° and 160°F. Undercooked meat can make people sick, so have an adult help make sure your worm is fully cooked!

MONSTER-HAND MEAT LOAF

A scrumptious severed hand made of meat, complete with frightening onion fingernails.

Ingredients

1½ pounds ground beef
1 egg
1 chopped onion
1 cup milk
1 cup dried bread crumbs
1 cup grated carrot
1 cup chopped spinach
¼ cup brown sugar
ketchup
¼ cup shredded cheese

Tools

- knife
- cutting board
- measuring cups
- grater
- large bowl
- large baking pan
- oven mitts
- meat thermometer

Serves: 4
Preparation Time: 1 hour, 20 minutes

1. Preheat the oven to 350°F. Put all the ingredients except the ketchup and shredded cheese in a large bowl. Save a handful of onion slices for later. Mix together the ingredients with clean hands.

1

2. In a large baking pan, form a hand with the meat mixture. Shape a large palm and wrist. Then form the fingers.

3. Place a slice of onion on the end of each finger to look like a fingernail.

4. Bake the hand for 40 minutes. Take the meat loaf out. Then decorate with ketchup and cheese to make it look like a supergross hand. Bake another 10 minutes, and check for doneness.

3

5. Place meat loaf hand on a serving dish, and add more ketchup. Then serve this horrifying hand to unsuspecting diners!

TIP

Ground beef is safe to eat at 160°F. Use a meat thermometer to make sure your monster hand is done.

4

BRAIN-CHUNK DUMPLINGS

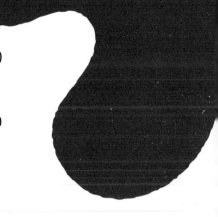

What do diners think of squiggly brain bits?
Find out as your guests dine on these delicious
dumplings!

Ingredients

Dumpling and Filling

8 ounces white mushrooms

2 baby bok choy

2 carrots

6 green onions

3 tablespoons grapeseed oil

3 cloves minced garlic

3 tablespoons freshly grated ginger

¼ cup soy sauce

2 tablespoons ketchup

¼ teaspoon salt

1 14-ounce package wonton
   wrappers

2 tablespoons cornstarch

Sauce

1 cup soy sauce

1 cup ketchup

¼ cup grapeseed oil

4 teaspoons freshly grated ginger

Tools

- knife
- cutting board
- large frying pan
- measuring spoons
- mixing spoons
- grater
- measuring cups
- mixing bowls
- baking sheet
- waxed paper
- whisk
- pastry brush
- paper towels
- 2 aluminum pie tins
- rolling pin
- screwdriver or scissors
- stockpot or saucepan
- 4–5 binder clips
- serving bowls

Serves: 4
Preparation Time: 1 hour

1. Chop the mushrooms, bok choy, carrots, and green onions into ¼ to ½-inch pieces.

2. With an adult's help, heat the oil in the frying pan over medium heat. Add the mushrooms, bok choy, carrots, and green onions. Cook for 5 to 7 minutes, stirring regularly.

3. Add the garlic, ginger, soy sauce, and ketchup, and cook for another 3 minutes. The liquid will begin to evaporate. Add the salt. Put all the cooked ingredients into a bowl. Then refrigerate for 20 minutes.

4. Line the baking sheet with a piece of waxed paper. Whisk together the cornstarch and 1 cup water.

5. Place two stacked wonton wrappers on the baking sheet. Brush the cornstarch mixture onto the top wrapper. Put a heaping teaspoon of filling in the middle. Fold the wrappers into a triangle and seal the edges. Trim the edge about ¼ inch from the filling pocket. This is your first brain!

6. Cover your first brain with a damp paper towel while you stuff more brains. Repeat steps 5 and 6 until you run out of wrappers or filling.

Brain-Chunk Dumplings continued next page

For a meaty meal, try mixing the veggie filling with 1 pound of ground pork or turkey.

Brain-Chunk Dumplings, continued

7 Now make a **steamer** with the pie tins. Poke sixteen to twenty holes in the bottom of each tin with a clean screwdriver or scissors. Be careful not to cut yourself on the holes' sharp edges. Next flatten one tin with a rolling pin.

8 Add about 2 inches of water to a stockpot, and bring to a boil over medium-high heat. With an adult's help, place the unflattened pie tin over the pot's opening. Add five to six wonton brains to the tin. Then place the flattened tin on top of the first tin.

9 With adult help, secure the tins' edges with binder clips. Be careful—the steam will be hot! Cook for 5 to 6 minutes. Repeat until all of the brains are cooked.

10 Stir the sauce ingredients together in a bowl. Then toss each brain in the sauce to coat it.

11 Divide your dumplings into serving bowls. Now sit back and watch your guests enjoy these dumpling brains!

WRAPPING UP

Cleaning Up

Once you are done cooking, it is time to clean up! Make sure to wipe up spills, wash dishes, and clear the table. Wash and put away any props you used that don't belong in the kitchen. Make sure any leftovers are properly packaged and refrigerated.

Keep Cooking!

Get inspired by your disgusting dinner creations. Dream up new ideas for gruesome, edible dishes. Or go back and make your own versions of the revolting recipes you tried. Think gross, and keep on cooking!

GLOSSARY

boil: liquid that has become so hot that bubbles form and rise to the top

broil: to cook by exposing a food directly to a heat source

capers: pickled flower buds often used in cooking

edible: something that can be safely eaten

garnish: to decorate food before serving it

minced: chopped or cut into very small pieces

pimientos: sweet peppers that are often chopped into small pieces and stuffed into olives

preheat: to heat an oven to the required temperature before putting in the food

sanitized: cleaned so something is free of germs

simmer: to cook something in water that is not quite boiling and has very small bubbles

steamer: a container in which food is cooked using steam

whisk: to stir very quickly using a fork or a tool made of curved wire, also called a whisk

FURTHER INFORMATION

Cook, Deanna F. *Cooking Class: 57 Fun Recipes Kids Will Love to Make (and Eat)!* North Adams, MA: Storey Publishing, 2015.
From popcorn chicken to mashed potatoes, this book gives you the basics you need to know to make delicious meals for your family.

Larson, Jennifer S. *Delicious Vegetarian Main Dishes.* Minneapolis: Millbrook Press, 2013.
Create some healthful, meat-free dinners using the tasty recipes in this book.

Spatulatta.com
http://www.spatulatta.com
With videos, blog posts, and more, this website has everything you need to get started in the kitchen.

Spooky Halloween Recipes
http://www.foodnetwork.com/recipes/photos/spooky-halloween-recipes-for-kids.html
Check out this website for even more scary recipes that are just right for Halloween or any time of year!

INDEX